FOOTBALL LEGENDS

Troy Aikman

Terry Bradshaw

Jim Brown

John Elway

Brett Favre

Michael Irvin

Vince Lombardi

John Madden

Dan Marino

Joe Montana

Joe Namath

Walter Payton

Jerry Rice

Barry Sanders

Deion Sanders

Emmitt Smith

Lawrence Taylor

Steve Young

CHELSEA HOUSE PUBLISHERS

FOOTBALL LEGENDS

VINCE LOMBARDI

John Wukovits

Introduction by
Chuck Noll

CHELSEA HOUSE PUBLISHERS
Philadelphia

Produced by Daniel Bial and Associates
New York, New York

Picture research by Alan Gottlieb
Cover illustration by Bill Vann

First Printing

1 3 5 7 9 8 6 4 2

Library of Congress Cataloging-in-Publication Data

Wukovits, John F., 1944-
        Vince Lombardi / John Wukovits; introduction by Chuck Noll.
          p.   cm. -- (Football legends)
        Includes bibiliographical references and index.
        ISBN 0-7910-4398-3
        1. Lombardi, Vince--Juvenile literature. 2. Football coaches--
United States--Biography--Juvenile literature. 3. Green Bay Packers
(Football team)--History--Juvenile literature. [1. Lombardi, Vince. 2. Football
coaches.]
I. Title. II. Series.
GV939.L6W85   1997
796.323'092--dc21
[B]
96-52616

        CIP

        AC

CONTENTS

A WINNING ATTITUDE

Chuck Noll

Don't ever fall into the trap of believing, "I could never do that. And I won't even try—I don't want to embarrass myself." After all, most top athletes had no idea what they could accomplish when they were young. A secret to the success of every star quarterback and sure-handed receiver is that they tried. If they had not tried, if they had not persevered, they would never have discovered how far they could go and how much they could achieve.

You can learn about trying hard and overcoming challenges by being a sports fan. Or you can take part in organized sports at any level, in any capacity. The student messenger at my high school is now president of a university. A reserve ballplayer who got very little playing time in high school now owns a very successful business. Both of them benefited by the lesson of perseverance that sports offers. The main point is that you don't have to be a Hall of Fame athlete to reap the benefits of participating in sports.

In math class, I learned that the whole is equal to the sum of its parts. But that is not always the case when you are dealing with people. Sports has taught me that the whole is either greater than or less than the sum of its parts, depending on how well the parts work together. And how the parts work together depends on how they really understand the concept of teamwork.

Most people believe that teamwork is a fifty-fifty proposition. But true teamwork is seldom, if ever, fifty-fifty. Teamwork is *whatever it takes to get the job done*. There is no time for the measurement of contributions, no time for anything but concentrating on your job.

One year, my Pittsburgh Steelers were playing the Houston

Oilers in the Astrodome late in the season, with the division championship on the line. Our offensive line was hard hit by the flu, our starting quarterback was out with an injury, and we were having difficulty making a first down. There was tremendous pressure on our defense to perform well—and they rose to the occasion. If the players on the defensive unit had been measuring their contribution against the offense's contribution, they would have given up and gone home. Instead, with a "whatever it takes" attitude, they increased their level of concentration and performance, forced turnovers, and got the ball into field goal range for our offense. Thanks to our defense's winning attitude, we came away with a victory.

Believing in doing whatever it takes to get the job done is what separates a successful person from someone who is not as successful. Nobody can give you this winning outlook; you have to develop it. And I know from experience that it can be learned and developed on the playing field.

My favorite people on the football field have always been offensive linemen and defensive backs. I say this because it takes special people to perform well in jobs in which there is little public recognition when they are doing things right but are thrust into the spotlight as soon as they make a mistake. That is exactly what happens to a lineman whose man sacks the quarterback or a defensive back who lets his receiver catch a touchdown pass. They know the importance of being part of a group that believes in teamwork and does not point fingers at one another.

Sports can be a learning situation as much as it can be fun. And that's why I say, "Get involved. Participate."

CHUCK NOLL, the Pittsburgh Steelers head coach from 1969–1991, led his team to four Super Bowl victories — the most by any coach. Widely respected as an innovator on both offense and defense, Noll was inducted into the Pro Football Hall of Fame in 1993.

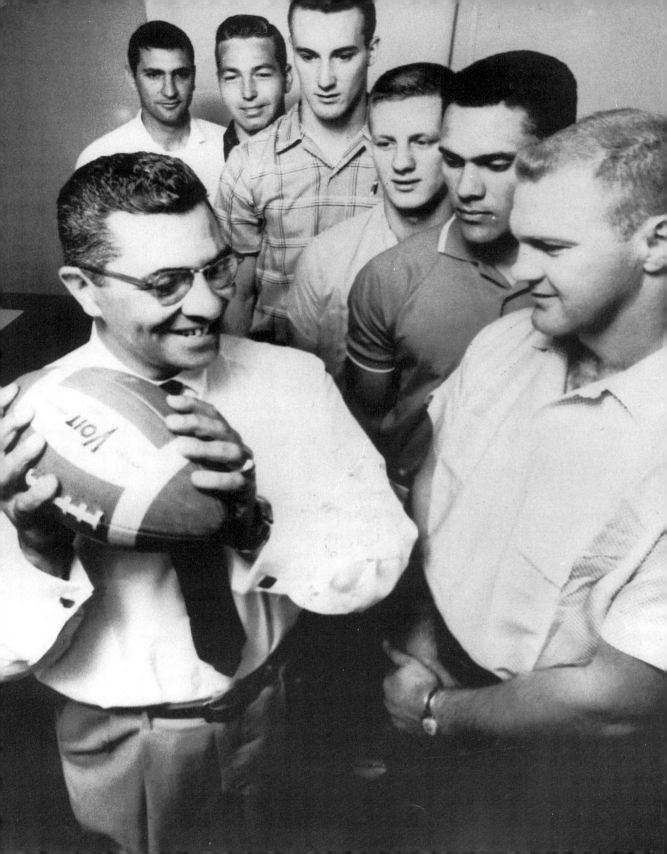

1
"THERE'S NO PLACE FOR A LOSER"

The returning veterans from the previous season's professional football team gathered in the Green Bay Packer lockerroom to hear the first talk delivered by their new coach. Versatile quarterback-running back Paul Hornung, fullback Jim Taylor, seldom-used quarterback Bart Starr, fun-loving and slightly out-of-shape end Max McGee, and others wondered what changes, if any, he would install.

They knew that some alterations would occur, for the current roster had brought few victories to the football-crazed fans of Green Bay, Wisconsin. Still, they were professionals, they had seen coaches come and go, and beyond a handful of face-saving switches, they expected little out of the ordinary.

"Gentlemen, this is a football." In 1959, Vince Lombardi had to create a team nearly from scratch. Candidates for quarterback included (from left to right): Babe Parilli, Bart Starr, Boyd Dowler, Bob Webb, Joe Francis, and Lamar McHan.

Though the forty-six-year-old Vince Lombardi was coaching his first professional team, he was no ordinary man. He understood that much had to be done to transform the ragtag group of individuals into a winning Green Bay Packer team, and he had a plan to earn the praise and devotion of its fans.

Begun in 1919 by Earl "Curly" Lambeau, the Packers had quickly developed a reputation for sound play and winning seasons. Recently, however, the team had flopped. The suffering population of Green Bay—some 63,000 people in 1959—had endured 11 straight losing seasons, capped by the horrendous 1958 record of one win, 10 losses, and one tie, the worst record in Packer history.

Lombardi had heard and read the taunts hurled in the team's direction and agreed with much of it. The previous year's squad had such poor discipline that they frequently fooled around during practices, came in late, and dressed in sloppy T-shirts and slacks when traveling to away games. Players visited the bars enough to anger one fan who wrote to the local newspaper asking why anyone should pay for a ticket to a game "when for the price of a drink you can see them practically any night on the town?"

Even a prominent national sports columnist had turned the Packers into a National Football League joke when he summarized the 1958 Packer season by writing they "overwhelmed one opponent, underwhelmed ten, and whelmed one."

Before he ever talked to his team, Lombardi spent hours with his staff watching film. In three months they studied 20,000 feet of film, evaluating the strengths and weaknesses of both offense and defense. While noticing an abundance of raw talent, Lombardi came away feeling somewhat distraught at the work that had to be done. He once emerged from the film room and remarked to his secretary, "I think I have taken on more than I can handle. Will you pray for me and help me?"

Lombardi wasted little time in trying to reach his players. "Gentlemen, I have never been with a losing team, " he said in a low voice. Then, allowing his voice to rise to a gruff shout, he added, "And I don't intend to be with a losing team now!" The force of his words caused every player to look squarely at their new coach.

Emphasizing each sentence with a pounding voice and steely eyes, Lombardi continued. "We're here to play big-league football. I'm going to bring a championship team to Green Bay, and I'm counting on every man in this room to do his job. I want total dedication from every man on this squad. I want every man dedicated to the only thing that's important in this league: winning the game."

Should any player wonder what the consequences for sloppy play or poor effort would be, Lombardi left no doubt. "I'm going to work you like you've never been worked before. I'm going

Lombardi's Packers featured great runners in Jim Taylor (left) and Paul Hornung.

to push and drive, drive and push. If you don't think you're a winner, you don't belong here!"

Shocked players heard words that nobody had ever used before, but their coach had only warmed up. "There is nobody big enough to think he's got the team made or can do what he wants. Trains and planes are going in and coming out of Green Bay every day, and he'll be on one of them. I won't."

He described the only type of individual he wanted on his team, one who would get himself "into shape mentally. I want you to ache to get back into action. I want players who are aggressive even when it hurts. I'm going to find thirty-six men [the then roster size] who have the pride to make any sacrifice to win."

Lombardi next rammed home his team rules. He insisted that players not simply be on time to practice, meetings, and meals but fifteen minutes early—which the players gradually began calling "Lombardi time." He explained that "a man who's late for meetings or the bus won't run his pass routes right. He'll be sloppy."

He declared certain Green Bay bars off limits and explained that when on trips for away games each man would wear a green sports coat with a gold Packer emblem on the breast pocket, with dress shirt and tie. They were professionals, he explained, and should begin acting and looking like professionals.

After explaining the fines for breaking rules, Lombardi concluded by saying, "There's no place on this team for a loser! I get paid to win! We're going to win!"

The numbed athletes filed out of the room, each with his own impression of what he had just heard. Some scoffed that they had heard tough talk before and that before long, conditions would return to normal. But linebacker Bill Forester was so excited, he said, "I could hardly sleep that night." Quarterback Bart Starr wondered, "Holy cow, where have you been all my life?"

The scoffers were soon to be dismissed from the team. The Green Bay Packers who remained were about to write football history.

2

"I ALWAYS WANTED IT MORE"

Born on June 11, 1913, Vincent Thomas Lombardi learned early in his life to face hard work with a smile. Lombardi ancestors fled southern Italy to escape miserably poor conditions, but could afford nothing more than to settle in a slum area labeled "Little Italy" in Brooklyn, New York. His father, Enrico, labored 11 hours a day in his butcher shop to lift the family from its humble origins, and gradually succeeded in moving to a more pleasant neighborhood in Englewood, New Jersey.

Enrico rarely missed a chance to drill into Vince and his two brothers, Joseph and Harold, that a man gets ahead by outworking everyone else and by performing his job properly. Each day after school, Vince rushed to his father's butcher shop where, as he lifted crates and moved stock, he listened to Enrico remind him,

Vince Lombardi only weighed 180 pounds when he played lineman at Fordham University. But his ferocity and intensity made him a great competitor.

"If you're going to do something, do it right and do it the first time."

One time Vince limped into the store to tell his father he was hurt playing football and could not work. Enrico stared at the youth, then firmly replied, "Hurt is in the mind. You've got to make yourself tough and you've got to play when it hurts. That's when you play best, when it hurts. If you don't want to get hurt, then don't play football." With an icy stare, he then added, "And you'd better work in the store today or else."

Religion also played an important role in the Lombardi family. Raised Roman Catholic, Vince flirted with the idea of becoming a priest, and in 1929 even enrolled in a Catholic high school that trained boys who were considering the priesthood. However, after his third year, he decided the religious life was not for him and switched to St. Francis Preparatory School in Brooklyn.

The move proved to be one of the most valuable Lombardi ever made, for here he met two men who helped establish his future in football—coach Harry Kane and teacher Dan Kern. Harry Kane, who had coached baseball immortal Lou Gehrig, hammered two essential ingredients of successful sports into his players—proper execution of fundamentals and giving everything you've got all the time.

Though small at 5'8" and 165 pounds and far from the most talented athlete on the squad, the solidly-built Lombardi turned into a tiger on the field, mainly through desire and by outhustling everybody. "I had this drive to be first, or best in everything," explained Lombardi. "I wasn't born with much size or speed, and so everything I did in the field of athletics was a struggle. I had to try harder than anyone else. But there is some-

thing to be said for that kind of an attitude, because I found that if I really wanted something badly enough, it was possible. I always tried to want it more than the other kids. That was my edge."

His all-out style of play intimidated opposing players. As a halfback, he relished charging straight at would-be tacklers to see if he could bowl them over, which he usually did. When the team needed one or two yards, the ball was normally placed in Lombardi's hands. Defensively, he tackled with such a vengeance that a teammate said, "When he hit you, you knew it."

He played both offense and defense every game, whether healthy or injured. A friend claimed, "You couldn't knock the guy out. He'd never give up." Lombardi's intense manner of playing on the field stunned Brother Edmund, his English teacher, who had seen only the classroom side of Vince. When he first saw Lombardi play, "I said to myself, 'This is two different people! In the classroom he's silent, polite, mannerly, but on the football field he's a terror!" Vince helped lead the team to the City Catholic High School Championship and earned a place on the All-City team.

The second man to influence Lombardi was his foreign language teacher, Dan Kern, with whom he spent hours discussing his future. Lombardi worried that lack of money and connections might keep him out of a good school, but Kern wrote a flattering letter about Lombardi to Jack Coffey, the athletic director at Fordham University. Kern boosted Vince's weight by 15 pounds, because "they wouldn't have looked at him if I said he was so low in weight," and Fordham decided to take a chance on the stocky lineman.

Fordham head coach Jim Crowley, who gained fame as one the legendary running backs of Knute Rockne's Four Horsemen and later became one of college football's most successful coaches, confirmed in Lombardi's mind that firm discipline and hard work brought success. Crowley ran brisk practices filled with constant drills and told his players that he wanted no "loafing, no halfhearted effort, no indifference either mental or physical, but hard, aggressive, brainy work from beginning to end."

Lombardi played little until his senior year because Fordham contained so much talent. Finally, under the guidance of line coach Frank Leahy, another man who would gain fame as coach at Notre Dame University, Lombardi blossomed into a valued member of an offensive line so adept at sweeping opponents out of the way that one national magazine writer labeled them the Seven Blocks of Granite. The seven stared across at the other team with the attitude, "We are ready to do or die. Are you?"

"At all times he was willing to pay any price," said Coach Leahy of Lombardi, "which included effort, blood, pain, and sacrifice." In one game Lombardi faced the massive Pittsburgh All-American, Tony Matisis, who outweighed Lombardi by 30 pounds. Though absorbing a horrible beating to his face from the vicious tackle, who smacked Lombardi across the mouth on almost every play, Lombardi kept him away from Fordham's running backs. Bleeding profusely from the mouth and in tremendous pain, Lombardi played the entire game without complaint, because he believed that pain was simply in a person's mind and could thus be controlled. Afterward, though, when a team physician sewed thirty stitches into Lombardi's gums to stem the bleeding, he did admit, "I was certainly hurting in my mind."

Though other players on the offensive line garnered the All-American honors over Lombardi, no one outhustled him. His effort earned an honorable mention on one national team and abundant praise from coaches.

Lombardi did not enjoy as much success in Fordham's classrooms, although he made he honor roll once and finished in the top 25% of his class. One person he met while at Fordham, Marie Planitz, became his lifelong companion. The shy Lombardi, who had never dated much in high school, was instantly struck by her beauty and quickly decided that she was the one for him. Marie agreed. "Suddenly he plopped into my life, and nothing was ever the same."

After graduating, Lombardi enrolled in Fordham's law school, but withdrew following one semester because he missed sports. While working for a finance company during the day, Lom-

In 1944, Lombardi's "Fighting Saints" of St. Cecilia High School had a record of 10-0-1.

bardi played semi-professional football on weekends for the Wilmington Clippers and other teams, but he was unhappy with his life.

Finally in 1939, after two disappointing years, Lombardi received the offer he was looking for. Andy Palau, coach and athletic director at St. Cecilia High School in Englewood, New Jersey, asked Vince to coach football, basketball, and baseball, as well as teach. A new door into the world of coaching had opened for the excited Lombardi, who charged through without ever looking back.

At first, Lombardi had trouble adjusting to high school because he expected so much from both players on the field and students in the classroom. His impatience exploded on numer-

ous occasions and frequently produced tears from the hapless target of his wrath. During one practice, an end repeatedly made the same mistake on a reverse play. An irate Lombardi charged up to him and let loose a torrent of words that so petrified the intimidated youth that he broke down in tears. Lombardi backed away, and later admitted he had been too hard on the boy. "I realized then that he was just a 17-year-old kid and we were asking the impossible."

He encountered the same reaction in the classroom, where he taught mainly physics and chemistry. As he did on the football field, Lombardi expected his students to be thoroughly prepared, good-mannered, and ready with each day's assignment. He drilled them constantly on the basics of the subject and never hesitated to let anyone know when he was not doing his job. As a result, students feared the stern teacher. One recalled that, "You didn't dare read a book or turn your head or look at the person next to you. He'd walk around that room like a tiger."

In the fifth game of his first season at St. Cecilia's, Palau asked his assistant to give the pre-game pep talk. His speech so electrified the crowd that Palau swore "the gymnasium shook," and one player stated that Lombardi would "get you so roused up, you'd run through a wall for the man."

On August 31, 1940, Lombardi married his sweetheart, then whisked her off to Maine. However, Lombardi, with his typical dedication, cut short the honeymoon so he could be back in time for the September 3 opening of fall practice. This must have hurt the new bride, but she gradually accepted that her husband's frequent absence was a facet of his personality that she must endure. She later warned the wife of another man thinking of getting into coaching that "you're not going to see him! Don't you understand?" Vince and Marie eventually had two children—Vincent, Jr., born on April 27, 1942, and Susan, born February 18, 1947.

When the Japanese attacked Pearl Harbor in December, 1941, Lombardi attempted to enlist in the service, but was rejected because of poor eyesight. In 1942, Lombardi took over the reins of the St. Cecilia program when Palau resigned as head coach. After losing his first game to Englewood, 18-7, Lombardi did not taste defeat until 1944 as his squad ran off a 32-game unbeaten streak.

As he would throughout his entire coaching career, Lombardi emphasized a sound execution of fundamentals, repetition of plays in practice, and avoidance of anything fancy. He wanted straight ahead football, the kind in which players blocked, runners ran, and defenders tackled with a vengeance. "I'll do all the thinking," Lombardi yelled at his players. "Just do exactly as I tell you. Don't improvise!"

One sportswriter described the powerful Lombardi teams of 1942-1944 as, "They just went out and beat the living heck out of you. They blocked and tackled you to death."

On game day, Lombardi delivered stirring pregame pep talks which sent his players onto the field like hungry tigers seeking prey. "Your mother and father are out there," he reminded them. "They're looking at you! Five thousand people will be looking at you!" Lombardi then stared into each player's eyes and shouted, "They'll be watching that block!" or "They'll be watching you run!"

He was an enigma. While pounding into his boys that "your moral integrity is the most priceless thing you possess" and showing he meant it by going to daily Mass, Lombardi would get so intense before some games that at Sunday church he would not even speak to his close friend, Red Gerrity, who coached rival Englewood High School. Before one crucial game, each St. Cecilia player received postcards from a Brooklyn opponent filled with insulting remarks about their talent. "Naturally, we got all fired up and went out and beat Brooklyn Prep," mentioned a player. Later, the team learned that Lombardi had written and mailed the postcards to fire up his team.

His tactics certainly produced champions. After an initial record of 6-1-2, St. Cecilia won every game in an 11-0 season during which they recorded eight shutouts and outscored their opponents, 267-29. He achieved similar results coaching the basketball squad, where he ran off a 23-game winning streak, won the state parochial school championship in 1945, and compiled an 111-51 record in eight years. Altogether, the hard-driven coach won six state championships in eight years in the two sports.

He so loved coaching at the high school that Lombardi always claimed, "There was fun in coaching then that I have not found since." However, with powerhouse teams like he produced, colleges could not fail but to cast their eyes in his direction. In 1947 his alma mater, Fordham, came calling, followed shortly after by one of the nation's finest programs—West Point.

Lombardi returned to Fordham to take over the freshman squad in the summer of 1947, but he found a program in complete disarray. The varsity had suffered through such a horrendous 1946 season that Lombardi bluntly asserted, "My St. Cecilia club can knock off what I've seen at Fordham."

He plunged into his duties with typical gusto, and while his freshmen showed promise by winning both their scheduled games, the varsity stumbled under an ineffective head coach. The team scored a measly 44 points in recording an abysmal 1-6-1 mark.

Lombardi moved up to the varsity along with his freshmen standouts for the 1948 season. Hopes ran higher than the year before, but the team simply lacked depth and continued to absorb defeats, although their record improved to 3-6.

In spite of the troubles, Lombardi's talent drew notice in other quarters. The head football coach of the Army team at West Point, the legendary Red Blaik, needed an assistant. Blaik, who had built a successful program at Dartmouth from 1933-1940, was recruited by West Point to restore the school to football prominence. Within three years of his hiring in 1941, Blaik had turned West Point into the nation's premier program. From 1944-1950, Army posted five undefeated seasons and captured two national championships while compiling a record of 57-3-4.

A friend mentioned Lombardi's name to Blaik, who agreed to see the Fordham coach. Within minutes after the interview began, Blaik later told others, "I knew Lombardi was different. Maybe it was just a hunch, I don't know, but there was a look about him. He seemed so eager, so determined. He had that special quality of being able to electrify a room. His eyes flashed, and he came alive when he started talking about football theory."

Blaik hired Lombardi on the spot for the 1949 season, and from the beginning the two developed a close relationship. Though Blaik guided the cadets through an undefeated season that year, Lombardi's fiery approach and intensity produced some hostile reactions.

In 1947, Lombardi returned to Fordham University, this time as backfield coach.

Red Blaik, the greatest football coach in West Point history, hired Lombardi as an assistant in 1949.

"He didn't quite have control of his emotions that first season," mentioned Blaik. "The cadet players didn't really understand him, his tremendous drive and pursuit of perfection."

Under Blaik's tutelage, Lombardi learned not only to corral his emotions, but discovered there was a world of football knowledge to master. For five seasons Lombardi absorbed as much information at the feet of his mentor as he could.

The two analyzed up to 4,000 feet of film together. Lombardi used to walk into Blaik's office, and without a greeting the head coach would present a problem for Lombardi to solve. "It's third down," he would say. "The ball is on your 30. You need four yards. They are in a seven-man defense with the halfback playing up close behind the strong side. What play will you call?"

Like Lombardi's father, Blaik insisted his players strive for perfection. Lombardi felt comfortable in such an atmosphere and loved barking at the athletes, "You don't do things right once in a while; you do them right all the time."

For the rest of his life, wherever Lombardi coached, he maintained ties with Blaik and frequently called for advice. "Nobody knew anything about football unless they knew the Colonel. He took me in and taught me everything I know. Not only football, but life, and how to handle men, and how to win."

If he needed a test in how to handle adversity, Lombardi received it in 1951 when West Point expelled 90 cadets for cheating on exams. As 37 of those cadets, including Blaik's son, played football, the team plummeted from the height of national prominence to football weakling overnight. West Point struggled to two wins in

1951 and four the next year, but Blaik and Lombardi taught the boys to hold their heads high and that, with supreme effort, they could turn things around.

The program returned to preeminence in 1953. According to Blaik, a key moment occurred early in the season when, after battling back against Northwestern University, the team lost in the game's final moments. Lombardi "sat in the dressing room afterward and cried, because one player had made a mistake that cost the game for a bunch of kids who had worked so hard to come from nowhere." The players were so impressed with Lombardi's reaction that they came out the following Monday with renewed determination, and did not lose another game that year.

With his reputation in football rising, Lombardi was bound to be noticed by professional teams sooner or later. The first professional team to contact him was the New York Giants, who offered Lombardi an assistant coach's position in 1954. Though he hated to leave West Point, he was drawn by the chance to work with the best. "I decided to go with the pros because I felt I could come closer to finding the perfect football player," he explained. That proved tougher than he imagined.

3

"INCHES SHORT AND SEVEN SECONDS TOO LONG"

The Giants surprised the football world when they hired the 39-year-old Jim Lee Howell in December, 1953. Though he had played eight seasons for the Giants from 1938-1946, his background in coaching was limited. He recognized this and decided to give his top assistant coaches most of the responsibility for fashioning the offense and defense. Lombardi thus stepped into a job that instantly handed him the authority to implement his system.

Howell put Lombardi in charge of the offensive backfield. By teaming Lombardi with his acclaimed defensive assistant, Tom Landry, Howell loved to brag that he had the "two smartest assistant coaches in football." While alike in their deep love for the game, Lombardi and Landry were as opposite as day and night in temperament and style.

After being named backfield coach of the New York Giants, Lombardi, left, posed with fullback Mel Triplett, quarterback Charley Conerly, and halfbacks Phil King and Alex Webster.

"You could hear Vince laughing or shouting for five blocks," claimed Vince's former Fordham classmate, team owner Wellington Mara. "You couldn't hear Landry from the next chair."

Lombardi had the ability to assess how badly each man wanted to play and how to draw out extra effort. Thus he employed different tactics with each man: he might put one player through a horrendous tongue-lashing, while dishing out compliments to another. Lombardi, one of the great motivators of all time, was a master at knowing what buttons to push to get different men to excel.

He especially worked wonders with the Giant backfield who, until Lombardi's arrival, functioned erratically. Seven-year veteran quarterback Charlie Conerly was an intelligent leader who showed great courage on the field, yet his unemotional approach gave the image that he did not care and subjected him to horrible booing by Giant fans. Conerly even considered retiring after the 1953 season.

Former All-American halfback Kyle Rote fit Lombardi's image of a superb player. Though slowed down because of serious knee injuries that required him to move to flanker, Rote compensated by running intelligent pass routes containing numerous feints. He also practiced catching the football until he could snare the pigskin with the best. A perfectionist like Lombardi, Rote seemed made for the new coach's system.

Frank Gifford, a versatile player whose smooth running abilities awed opponents, excelled on both offense and defense. Frequently playing entire games, however, exhausted the former All-American back from USC. After losing 20 pounds during the 1953 season, a weary Gifford, like Conerly, considered retiring.

These men quickly changed their minds when Lombardi arrived. The new offensive coach's first words to Gifford as the star player arrived in training camp were, "Hi, I'm Vince Lombardi, and you're my halfback." Elated that he would be used solely on offense, Gifford dropped the notion of retiring. "They were the most important words anybody ever said to me in football," explained Gifford. "I had never been anyone's halfback."

Lombardi coached in the NFL the same way he formerly taught in St. Cecilia's classrooms—he took complicated material and presented it simply, then repeated it over and over until the information stuck in his players' heads.

Lombardi's style breathed fresh air into Conerly and Gifford. In one game, Conerly broke his nose, but instead of coming off the field, the bloody quarterback continued playing, even though he twice had to call time-outs so trainers could push his nose back into place. Lom-

In the fourth quarter of the 1958 championship game, Mel Triplett (number 33) battled across the goalline despite the best efforts of Art Donovan (number 70) and many other Baltimore Colts. The Giants, however, could not hold the lead and eventually lost in overtime in what has been called the greatest game ever played.

bardi later praised his quarterback by stating, "I've never coached a football player who had more courage."

Gifford blossomed under Lombardi. In 1956, instead of being retired, he was named the NFL's Player of the Year.

Together with the superb play of defensive back Emlen Tunnell and stocky fullback Alex Webster, the trio of Gifford, Conerly, and Rote led the Giants back into the winning column. While Lombardi worked his magic with the offense, Landry refashioned the defense. The team strung together two winning seasons in a row before capturing the 1956 NFL championship with a 47-7 thrashing of the Chicago Bears.

In 1958, Lombardi coached in one of football's most memorable games. After capturing their conference title, the Giants faced the Baltimore Colts in the NFL championship game. Baltimore punched through New York's defense for two touchdowns to take a 14-3 halftime lead. In the third quarter, the Giants rallied for a spectacular goal-line stand when it appeared that quarterback Johnny Unitas would take his team in for a third score. Then they took over on offense. Lombardi's unit swept the length of the field to close the gap to 14-10. They scored again early in the fourth quarter to take a 17-14 lead.

After stopping the Colts on successive drives, the Giants got the ball back. On third and four on their own 40 yardline and the clock falling under the three minute mark, Gifford was pulled to the ground inches shy of the first down marker by Gino Marchetti, even though the Colt defender broke his leg on the play.

Still, the Giants' lead seemed safe when punter Don Chandler pinned the Colts inside their own

20 with only 1:56 showing on the clock. Lombardi, confident that the defense could contain the Colts, "was sure that it was all over."

He had not counted on the spectacular leadership of Johnny Unitas, however. With an unerring arm, Unitas shredded the Giant defense and quickly moved his team to the New York 14. With seven seconds left in regulation, Steve Myhra kicked a field goal to knot the score at 17. The two teams headed into the first sudden death contest in NFL championship history.

The Giants won the coin toss, but again fell inches short of a key first down. Unitas worked his magic again and marched his team to the 1 yardline. Alan Ameche crashed into the end zone to complete the nail-biting contest, which many have called the greatest game ever played.

Tom Landry claimed that this game "marked the time, the game, and the place where pro football really caught on." Lombardi agreed, but could not accept the defeat with as much composure. He called it "the most disappointing moment of my years with the Giants. We had it won, and we gave it away." The game, he mentioned many times in his life, "was a couple of inches too short and seven seconds too long."

College football had long been more popular across America than pro football, and both were eclipsed by the popularity of baseball. But with this titanic struggle, the popularity of pro football began an ever-rising arc.

In 1960, Tom Landry left the Giants to start a 28-year stint as coach of the Dallas Cowboys. Before the start of the 1959 season, however, Lombardi was in Green Bay, Wisconsin, to take the reins of leadership of his first pro team.

4

"WINNING IS GAINED THROUGH DISCIPLINE"

At his first press conference as head coach and general manager of the Packers, the 45-year-old Lombardi told assembled reporters, "I will put winning above all else here. Winning is gained through discipline."

For over three months Lombardi and his staff analyzed thousands of feet of film to list the team's strengths and weaknesses. Based upon what he saw, Lombardi switched players to new positions. He and his coaches then devised game plans intending to take advantage of each opponent's weaknesses.

Lombardi's tough words were not just hot air. On the first day of practice, stars and non-stars were worked until they dropped. Tackle Henry Jordan noted that, "He treated us all the same—like dogs." When Lombardi noticed any player walking during that initial practice, he shouted,

Vince Lombardi bought a house for his wife, daughter Susan and son Vince, Jr. when they moved to Green Bay, Wisconsin.

"Run! Run! If you want to walk, you don't belong here."

One player, in particular, became the object of Lombardi's wrath. Paul Hornung, nicknamed the "Golden Boy," was a gifted athlete. But the handsome halfback also loved fine food and good times, and Lombardi had to fine him frequently for breaking curfew. Lombardi once ripped into him for sloppy habits and once asked angrily, "What do you want to be, Hornung, a playboy or a football player?"

In reality, Lombardi admired Hornung as much as any player he coached because Hornung came through in the clutch. "Any time you got down near the goal line," said Lombardi, "you gave the ball to Paul, because he'd get it in there somehow." Lombardi also recognized that the other players looked up to Paul, and if he as the new coach could handle Hornung, the others would fall in place.

Lombardi's grueling practices "almost killed us," stated Bart Starr, but the players quickly began the slow adjustment to life under a coach who expected perfection on every play. "Nobody vomited after a couple of days," mentioned assistant coach Phil Bengtson.

"You are preparing yourself mentally," Lombardi instructed them. "It is tough now, but when the other team quits in the fourth quarter and you're still strong, you'll thank me."

An offensive end did not feel like thanking him, and once complained to Lombardi's wife that her husband was too tough. She glanced at the player without sympathy and calmly replied, "How would you like to live with him?"

Lombardi wasted no time in practice. He and the coaches not only showed how to execute each play, but focused on the reasons why each block had to be done a certain way. According to quarterback Lamar McHan, "All of a sudden it was like a road map that was clear. I felt when I went on the field I had some solid ideas to work with."

Lombardi promised them that if they worked hard, they would see results, but if they did not, their stay would be very brief. "Don't cross me now. If it happens once, maybe it will go by. But if any one of you crosses me a second time, you're gone."

He traded the second-leading receiver in Packer history before training camp even began to prove his point. No one doubted the player's talent, but he carried a reputation as a troublemaker who did not put forth full effort.

He traded older members for younger ones and purged the team of anyone with a losing attitude. He brought in men like guard Fuzzy Thurston, defensive end Willie Davis, and defensive tackle Henry Jordan, men who had played on championship teams and knew what it took to win.

As the season drew nearer, fans raised their expectations for Lombardi's first squad, but the coach secretly had his doubts. He told close friends that he would be happy to win four games.

The Packers opened the regular season on September 27, 1959, in a home contest against their

Lombardi got his rookies to push harder by yelling at them as they practiced blocking.

archrival, the Chicago Bears. The Packers started with a flourish by recovering a Bear fumble of the opening kickoff. On their first offensive play, halfback Paul Hornung ran to the left, suddenly stopped, and tossed a perfect pass to wide-open receiver Lew Carpenter near the end zone. The home crowd rose to its feet to celebrate a certain score, then slumped with a groan when Carpenter dropped the ball. When Hornung missed a short field goal attempt a few plays later, fans wondered if this could be the old Packers all over again.

The teams went into the halftime lockerroom with the Bears leading, 3-0. Rather than criticize the team, which Lombardi might have done had this been practice, he praised them for moving the ball so well. They simply failed to punch it through into the end zone. He then added in a rising voice, "And now, men of Green Bay, step aside, make way for the mightiest Green Bay team in years. A winning team! Go get 'em, Green Bay!" With a tremendous roar, the players poured out onto the field.

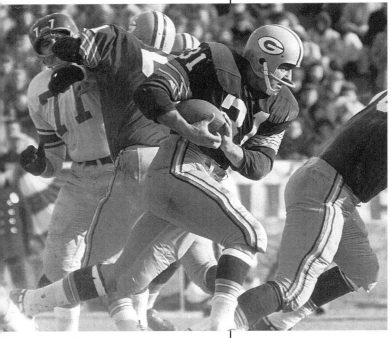

Jim Taylor's rushing helped the Packers win the 1961 NFL championship game against Lombardi's old team, the Giants.

Neither team scored in the third quarter. The Bears added a second field goal early in the fourth quarter to up their lead to 6-0.

Finally, a long pass to end Max McGee set up a scoring scamper by Jim Taylor, and the Packers grabbed their first lead of the young season.

Not long after, defensive back Dave Hanner charged through the Bear offensive line and tackled the Bear runner in the end zone for a safety to give the Packers a three-point lead, 9-6.

The Green Bay defense held off last-minute attempts by the Bears, and with the hometown fans shouting with glee, the players hoisted Lombardi to their shoulders and ran off with the victory. The next day, signs blanketed Green Bay proclaiming, "LOMBARDI FOR MAYOR!"

As can happen with an inexperienced club, the Packers rattled off victories and losses in streaks. They followed their opener with two more wins, then tumbled into a five-game stretch where they could not beat anyone.

During the losses, Lombardi once became so frustrated with their poor play that he gathered the team at practice for a chat. "You forgot every basic fundamental about this game," he yelled. "We are going to have to start all over again, from scratch." Lombardi then picked up a football and muttered, "Gentlemen, the basics. First of all, this is a football."

Before Lombardi could add another sentence, Max McGee broke the stillness. "Hang on a minute, Coach, you're going too fast." Everyone, including Lombardi, burst into laughter, then participated in some of the best practices of the year.

To snap his team out of its five-game stupor, Lombardi made one of the wisest moves of his career. Rather than alternating the quarterback position from Lamar McHan to Bart Starr, he made Starr the number one play-caller. This breathed fresh life into the squad, who swept to victories in their final five games to end the season at 7-5, an amazing turnaround from the dismal year before.

More than 7,500 jubilant fans greeted the Packers on December 14 when they returned from their final game, a 36-14 drubbing of San Francisco. Lombardi enjoyed the hero's welcome, but knew that much work yet remained.

"We should have won more games, but the people on this team just aren't accustomed to winning. They don't think like winners; they think they were lucky. That'll change. We have the makings here. I need some replacements, and I need to convince the rest of them that they are supposed to win."

Lombardi labored hard during 1960 preseason practices and games to instill a winning attitude in his players. When the team swept through its regular schedule with an 8-4 record to capture the Western Conference title, Lombardi appeared to have succeeded. In two short years, he had lifted the Packers from doormat to champions.

They met Philadelphia in December in the NFL championship game. Though the Eagles had a 10-2 record, the Packers stood as the favorite because of their stronger schedule.

Green Bay jumped out to a 6-0 lead, but Philadelphia quickly responded when cagey veteran quarterback Norm Van Brocklin hit flanker Tommy McDonald for a touchdown pass. A field goal shortly after vaulted Philadelphia into the lead, 10-6.

Green Bay regained the lead in the third quarter on a long drive that ended in a touchdown pass from Starr to McGee. Van Brocklin immediately responded with a touchdown drive to lift his team back on top, 17-13.

With only 1:20 showing on the clock, Green Bay got the ball on its own 35. Methodically,

Starr moved his team down the field until, with 22 seconds remaining, the Packers stood on the Eagle 20 yardline. As Hornung had missed a short field goal attempt just before the first half ended, Lombardi had no choice but to go for a touchdown, but on fourth down, linebacker Chuck Bednarek tackled Jim Taylor nine yards shy of the end zone to hand Green Bay a bitter 17-13 defeat.

A disappointed Lombardi explained that his team had made too many mistakes, particularly in not scoring more than three points after early Eagle turnovers. "I thought I had them ready," he said. "I'll just have to work harder."

When he heard that Lombardi planned to make 1961 even tougher on his men, Willie Davis wondered, "How can he make it any tougher? It's just not possible. But," he added with a sigh of resignation, "I know he will."

He did. His men had tasted a championship game; he now wanted them to dominate one. Thus his training camp asked more from the players than before. "I think Coach was afraid we'd play complacent football," mentioned Willie Davis. "My God, wouldn't he know we were more afraid of him than of any team?"

The team manhandled opponents all season long to tally an 11-3 record and gain a second Western Conference championship. The potent offense scored 391 points, and 12 players were named to the All-Pro team.

The players credited their success to Lombardi's brutal workouts, which molded them into exquisite physical specimens. "There are two kinds of conditioning," explained Henry Jordan. "The kind the other teams get and the Lombardi kind of conditioning. What is Lombardi conditioning? It's playing a full game, and not even perspiring in the fourth quarter, when the other guys are huffing and puffing, and their eyes are getting glassy."

Lombardi needed no incentive to get ready for the 1961 NFL championship game, as the opponent was his former team. "Just to play the Giants for the championship was more than I dared hope would happen," he said.

The Giants sported a bruising attack of its own, anchored upon the stellar play of veteran quarterback Y. A. Tittle, wide receiver Dale Shofner, hard-hitting linebacker Sam Huff, and a brutal defensive line called the "Fearsome Foursome."

The game was no contest. The Packers were forced to punt on their opening drive, but that was the only time that day they had to punt. By halftime they had a heady 24-0 lead, which they widened to 37-0 by game's end. Paul Hornung led the way offensively with 19 points, while the Packer defense slammed the door shut on the Giants and only permitted five first downs.

"It was the most awesome thing I've ever been involved in," said Giant tackle Greg Larson. "We had no way to stop them. They were like wild men."

Lombardi wasted little time savoring his first professional championship. He wanted more. As famed sports columnist Red Smith wrote, Vince's "wants are simple, merely to win every preseason exhibition, every game during the season, every postseason game, and every title. Give him that, and he'll ask for nothing else."

He practically accomplished the feat in 1962. From day one of training camp, Lombardi reminded his players that, "Once you're on top, everybody wants to knock you off. This is the real test. This year you find out whether or not you're really champions." He often used the phrase with which he is most associated, that "Winning isn't everything; it's the only thing."

Some have criticized this philosophy as condoning cheating, or putting too much pressure on athletes. But that's not what Lombardi meant at all. In fact, the words he preferred to use were, "Winning isn't everything—but making the effort to win is." He wanted his players to give more effort than they thought possible and to develop a winning attitude. Winning was important as a goal, something that gave meaning to pain and hard work. "I sure as heck didn't mean for people to crush human values and morality," he explained to a sportswriter.

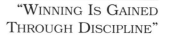

Emlen Tunnell initially had difficulty finding a hotel room when he reported to the Packers. One call from Lombardi, though, solved the problem.

Still, he continued to come down hard on his favorite player, Paul Hornung. Before one game in Chicago, Lombardi walked into a restaurant with some friends and spotted Hornung at the bar, accompanied by a beautiful date. As one of the coach's rules was never to drink the night before a game, Lombardi exploded and, in front of everyone, shouted to Hornung, "That'll cost you $500!" After his halfback stormed out, Lombardi tasted the drink and discovered it was only ginger ale, but he still made Hornung pay a fine for being out.

The Packers continued to respond to Lombardi's inspiration, increasing their streak to 18 wins in a row over two years, counting preseason and postseason play, before falling to the Detroit Lions on Thanksgiving Day. Lombardi even turned this defeat into an advantage by telling his players not to dwell on the loss. "The real glory is being knocked to your knees and then coming back."

Lombardi was as concerned with his players off the field as he was on. When Emlen Tunnell, a black, joined the team, he had difficulty finding living quarters. Tunnell pointed this out to Lombardi, who asked, "You mean you don't know where to stay?"

Lombardi telephoned Green Bay's nicest hotel, mentioned that one of his players needed a room, and said he wanted a special rate for the man. Then he added, more as an order than a question, "Oh, yes. The player is a Negro. That won't make any difference to you, will it?" Tunnell got his room and wound up enjoying his stay.

The Packers ended the season with three victories and claimed the conference championship with an enviable 13-1 record. Once again, they faced the Giants for the NFL crown. Smarting from the crushing defeat one year earlier, the Giants vowed revenge. One mentioned, "If we win this game, it won't be enough. We have to destroy the Packers and Lombardi."

A blustery, cold wind whipped across the Yankee Stadium field the entire game and all but took the passing attack away from both teams.

Since Hornung was just returning from a serious injury, the brunt of the Packer attack fell on Jim Taylor's massive legs. Though he responded gallantly, a combination of the Giant defense and a slippery field made him scratch and claw for every inch. The Packers would gain 10 or 15 yards, then punt to the Giants, who enjoyed no more success in the miserable conditions than Green Bay.

The game boiled down to football's basic elements—man against man, and each player against the cold. The Packers, trained by Lombardi to physically outlast the other team, rose to the test.

"It was this game," said Taylor, "that showed me the value of working under Coach Lombardi all those years before. I think he knew something like this was going to come to us, and he had us prepared for it. He taught us to withstand pain, and he taught us that if we can hold out, the other team will crack first."

The Packers wore down the Giants, and behind Taylor's gutsy performance, walked off with a hard-fought 16-7 victory. For the second year in a row, Lombardi's men were world champions.

Lombardi was hardly in awe at having won back-to-back titles. "Bubba," he mentioned to linebacker Bill Forester the day after defeating the Giants, "it's never been done three years in a row." One or two championships made most coaches' careers. Lombardi looked upon it as a start.

5

"PLAYING ON SUNDAY WAS THE EASIEST PART"

Winning a third straight championship, something never before done in NFL history, would be doubly hard, because earlier in 1963 the NFL commissioner, Pete Rozelle, indefinitely suspended star running back Paul Hornung for gambling on NFL games.

The Packers stumbled in an opening 10-3 loss to the Bears, but then ran off eight straight victories before again meeting Chicago. Tied for the conference lead with Green Bay at 8-1, the Bears had little trouble in a 26-7 win over the Packers. Though they finished the year with the NFL's second-best record at 11-2-1, the Packers finished behind 11-1-2 Chicago and sat out post-season play.

Though many observers picked the Packers to once again claim a championship in 1964, the

Bart Starr (number 15) threw for 4 touchdowns in the Packers' win over the Dallas Cowboys in the 1967 NFL championship game. Offensive line greats Jerry Kramer (64) and Fred Thurston (63) made sure Starr had enough time to throw.

Packers lost four of their first seven games to drop from the hunt. Their 8-5-1 final record left Lombardi feeling disappointed.

With Hornung's suspension lifted at last, and with several promising new players, Lombardi vowed a different outcome for 1965. "Two years in a row is too long for us to have been left out of championship games. We will win it this season."

The Green Bay of old returned as the Packers swept their first six games, then finished the season in a tie with the Baltimore Colts at 10-3-1. The Packers were heavy favorites to defeat Baltimore in the playoff game since both their superb quarterback, Johnny Unitas, and his replacement, were out with injuries. Colt coach Don Shula had to fall back upon halfback Tom Matte, who had played quarterback in college.

The undermanned Colts caught the Packers by surprise and, behind a physical defense, battled to a 10-10 tie in regulation. When Don Chandler saved the game by kicking a 32-yard field goal in sudden death, Lombardi breathed a sigh of relief and looked to the NFL title game against the Cleveland Browns. With Paul Hornung rushing for 105 yards, the Packers posted a 23-12 win for their first crown since 1962.

For 1966, NFL owners added a new wrinkle that would eventually grow into one of sport's hugest attractions—the Super Bowl. To eliminate the costly bidding war with the rival American Football League, NFL owners agreed to a merger, and pitted the two league champions in the Super Bowl.

Lombardi drove his men in each practice so they could reach the Super Bowl, and they responded by winning seven of the first eight games. As Bart Starr explained, "Lombardi never accepted compromise, with himself or his players. He would drive us all week until there was nothing that could be unexpected, and the playing on Sunday would be the easiest part of the week."

As the season unfolded, the Packers appeared to get stronger. They won their final five games to post an excellent 12-2 mark, and only missed an unbeaten season by four points. The NFL title game against Tom Landry's Dallas Cowboys almost sent Lombardi into convulsions. The teams traded scores all game long and approached the final three minutes with Green Bay clinging to a 34-27 lead.

Lombardi was a great believer in watching game film to discover the weaknesses of the opposing team.

Deftly blending short runs with passes, Cowboy quarterback Don Meredith led his team steadily toward the Packer end zone. With just under two minutes to play, Meredith lofted a pass toward the goal line. Packer safety Tom Brown was called for pass interference, which placed the ball on the Green Bay 2 yardline.

After a running play gained one yard, Meredith rolled out, spotted an open receiver, and spiraled the ball directly toward the man—who dropped the ball. An off-sides penalty against Dallas would have nullified any score, but seeing his defense collapse only made Lombardi's agony worse.

On second down and six yards to go, Meredith handed off to running back Don Perkins, who faked a run, then shocked the Packers by throw-

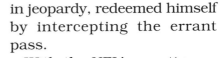

ing to a wide-open Dan Reeves in the end zone. He, too, dropped the ball.

A third down pass moved the Cowboys to the 2. On fourth down, linebacker Dave Robinson charged through the Dallas line and forced Meredith to throw his pass a moment too soon. Tom Brown, whose interference had put the team in jeopardy, redeemed himself by intercepting the errant pass.

With the NFL's prestige on the line, most every team owner or league official put pressure on Lombardi to win the Super Bowl. Lombardi grumbled that, "We had everything to lose and nothing to gain," but he had his team ready for the January 15, 1967 game in Los Angeles against the Kansas City Chiefs. The Chiefs, coached by Hank Stram, were assumed to be heavily outclassed by Lombardi's legions. The game started in that fashion when Bart Starr, on Green Bay's second possession, lifted a 37-yard touchdown pass to Max McGee.

The Chiefs stormed back, then continued to apply pressure on the Packers during the first half. In the second quarter, quarterback Len Dawson spotted Curtis McClinton alone in the end zone and hurled a 7-yard scoring strike to knot the score.

Even though Green Bay led at halftime, 14-10, Packer fans were worried. Rather than rolling over, the Chiefs had actually gained more yards than Lombardi's offense. Lombardi decided in the

Elijah Pitts, after taking the ball from Bart Starr (15), followed the blocking of Jerry Kramer (64) and Fred Thurston (63) during the Packers' victory in Super Bowl I.

lockerroom to blitz—send his linebackers charging through in an effort to tackle the quarterback or disrupt the flow of the play. Though Lombardi normally preferred a more conservative style of defense, he felt he had to take a gamble.

It paid off, as the Packers shut down Dawson and the Kansas City offense. The team rolled to a 35-10 victory. Lombardi celebrated his second consecutive championship and history-making first Super Bowl victory.

Though he coached the oldest team in the league, with 10 players starting at least their tenth season, and although Paul Hornung and Jim Taylor retired before the season, Lombardi knew how to motivate his team for 1967. "Gentlemen," he said, "no team in the history of the National Football League has ever won three straight world championships. If you succeed, you will never forget this year for the rest of your lives."

Six victories in the first seven games placed the Packers atop the league, mainly through Lombardi's knack of getting more out of his players. As Hornung had always loved saying, "Coach has a way of getting extra out of a player. If he told me to run into the stands and start selling programs, I wouldn't even question it. I'd be sure we'd get a touchdown out of it, somehow."

Though the Packers posted a 9-4-1 record, they lost their final two games and had to face the Los Angeles Rams in a playoff to determine the Western Conference championship. The confident Rams, winner of eight in a row, taunted the older Packers as being a team of the past. Lombardi stapled news clippings of these comments onto the lockerroom bulletin board, and a fired-up Packer unit crushed the Rams, 28-7.

A rematch with Dallas next awaited the Packers. Miserable Green Bay weather—including below zero temperatures and brisk winds—greeted the teams the day of the game. Frank Gifford, covering the game as a television broadcaster, said it was so cold that "I remember putting down a paper cup of coffee on the TV booth counter. A few minutes later I picked it up, and it had frozen solid."

Dallas expected Green Bay to avoid the wind and keep the ball on the ground, but Lombardi surprised them by having Starr take to the air. He completed four passes in the opening drive, the last of which resulted in a touchdown to receiver Boyd Dowler. Starr followed that with a 43-yard scoring toss to increase Green Bay's lead to 14-0, a seemingly comfortable lead in such horrible weather.

However, Dallas stormed back. They ran in a Starr fumble for a touchdown, then added a field goal to draw within four points. Following a scoreless third quarter, Dallas tallied on a trick pass from halfback Dan Reeves to grab the lead, 17-14.

As the temperature dropped dangerously low and strong winds stung players' faces, Green Bay received the ball with under five minutes remaining. They had to either score now or hope for a miracle.

Green Bay players summoned the strength and desire for one more drive. Lombardi had pounded into their heads that the winner in a bitter contest would be whichever team wanted it more, and now they did precisely that. Jerry Kramer stated that, "Some of us old heads got together. We decided we'd play for the old man. All of us love him. We didn't want to let him down.

Every guy made up his mind that we were going to go down swinging."

Utilizing his running backs and his receivers, Starr moved the Packers ever closer in a frantic race against the clock. By the time the official whistled the two-minute warning, the Packers stood on the Dallas 30 yardline.

A pass and a run advanced the ball to the 1. With less than a minute to go, Lombardi could have gone for the tie with a field goal, but he wanted to put the game away. On first and goal, rookie running back Donnie Anderson was tackled for no gain. As the seconds ticked away, Anderson attempted another run—and again gained nothing.

Lombardi called time out with only 16 seconds remaining. He knew that if a third running play failed, time would expire and Dallas would rush off as victor. A field goal would send the game into sudden death, but Lombardi never even considered it. In a do-or-die situation, Starr kept the ball on a quarterback sneak behind Jerry Kramer and plunged into the end zone.

As in the previous year, the Super Bowl became almost an afterthought when compared to the drama of the Dallas-Green Bay bloodfests. The Packers easily handled the Oakland Raiders in Miami, Florida, 33-14. Lombardi had his third consecutive championship and people would have to consider his teams among the best ever.

In 1968, Donnie Anderson scored a touchdown to help Green Bay win its second Super Bowl and third consecutive championship.

6

"I THINK, 'WHAT WOULD LOMBARDI DO?'"

As the years passed, Lombardi became more concerned that the intense pressures of being both head coach and general manager were taking their toll on his health. Thus in February, 1968, he stepped down as head coach. Lombardi continued as general manager, but turned over the coaching job to his assistant, Phil Bengtson.

Lombardi had put together an amazing record in his nine seasons: his overall record of 98-30-4 included two Super Bowl victories, five NFL championships, and six Western Conference titles. Four times he received coach of the year honors. Illustrative of his talent for winning the big games, Lombardi won nine of 10 postseason games.

Lombardi enjoyed his retirement until the next football season, when he realized how badly he missed being involved with the on-field operations. During the first practice under Bengtson,

In 1969, Lombardi briefly came out of retirement to coach the Washington Redskins.

Lombardi watched from off to the side and later told a friend, "I knew right then, that I had made a horrible mistake."

Instead of prowling the sidelines, yelling at players to put out more effort, he sat in a luxury box far removed from the action. "It's murder," he commented. "I never knew I'd miss it as much."

Lombardi found the duties of general manager dull compared to the excitement on the field. "Hot dogs!" he once exclaimed. "How the heck many ways can you buy and sell hot dogs?" While he refused to interfere in any coaching decisions out of loyalty to Bengtson, Lombardi agonized when the team slipped to a 6-7-1 record.

Slowly, word leaked that Lombardi might be open to other coaching offers. While rejecting most, the one he received during the next Super Bowl from the president of the Washington Redskins, Edward Bennett Williams, was too tempting to ignore. When Williams offered him not only the duties as head coach and general manager, but threw in part ownership of the team, Lombardi announced his return to coaching on February 1, 1969.

Most football enthusiasts welcomed the news, though many fans in Green Bay felt betrayed. One man reacted, "I feel he's cheating us. We had him before anyone knew his name. He gave us the years of glory with the Packers. I understand why he wants to leave, but I don't know if I can forgive him for doing it. He belongs to Green Bay."

Lombardi plunged into his new job with typical enthusiasm. One of the first meetings he held was with veteran quarterback, Sonny Jurgensen, who had always mixed high living off the gridiron with great talent on the field. Lombardi told

Jurgensen he expected leadership from him and that as coach, he would be tougher on Jurgensen than on anyone else. His first order was for his quarterback to lose the trademark pot belly.

Jurgensen relished the fresh approach. The Redskins lacked discipline and suffered from inadequate coaching, which obviously led to disaster in games. "We were always disorganized," claimed Jurgensen of the 5-9 1968 season. "We were always making up plays in the huddle."

In his first training camp meeting, Lombardi let the team know he would not accept losing ways. "I have never been with a loser, and I do not think I'm ready to start at this time in my career. I am going to push you and push you and push you because I get paid to win and so do you."

He backed up his message in various ways. He, of course, put the men through the most rigorous training camp they had ever experienced. When one veteran fullback continued to make the same error time after time, and then arrived late for a meeting, Lombardi verbally tore into him in front of the entire squad, then cut him on the spot.

At the same time, the players realized that if they followed Lombardi's system, success would not be far behind. Jurgensen said, "I learned to love that man. I also learned more in my first five days of listening to him than I did in 12 years of listening to other coaches."

The Lombardi touch produced immediate results. For the first time in 14 years, the Redskins compiled a winning mark at 7-5-2. Washington fans, more accustomed to sloppy play and losing seasons, looked to 1970 with renewed enthusiasm.

One year was all they were to have with Lombardi, however. During a four-day pretraining camp, Lombardi felt so weak while running up a hill near his home that he could not reach the top, something he had always achieved with ease. When he almost collapsed during a social gathering, Lombardi decided to enter Georgetown University Hospital for tests.

During exploratory surgery on June 27, doctors removed a two-foot cancerous section of his colon. Though Lombardi said to Marie, "I'll beat this. I'm gonna beat this thing," doctors were less optimistic. He was sent home on July 10 to continue his recovery, but he experienced such horrible pain that he returned for additional surgery. On July 27, physicians discovered that the cancer had rapidly spread to other parts of Lombardi's body. They could do nothing to help the dying coach other than make his last days as comfortable as possible.

Marie at first wanted to keep the news from leaking to the public because, "I had shared him for years. This is one thing I'm not going to share." After the second operation, however, the illness could not be hidden. Friends in and out of football called or traveled to Washington to visit their old coach. Lombardi mentioned to one visitor, a Catholic priest, that "I'm not afraid to meet my God now. But what I do regret is that there is so much left to be done on earth.'

By mid-August, Lombardi began to slip in and out of consciousness. On August 31, Marie's and his 30th wedding anniversary, he regained consciousness long enough to open his eyes, look at Marie, and whisper, "Happy anniversary. Remember, I love you."

Four days later, Vince Lombardi died at the age of 57. An enormous throng of 3,000, including the six surviving members of the Seven Blocks of Granite, packed St. Patrick's Cathedral in New York City for the funeral Mass, while another 1,000 stood outside, hoping to get a glimpse as the casket was carried by. After eulogies by Terence Cardinal Cooke and Bart Starr, 40 limousines slowly followed the hearse on its way to the cemetery.

Tributes and flattering words poured in. Sonny Jurgensen muttered, "I envy all those guys from Green Bay. They had Vince for nine years. We only had him for one, just long enough for him to educate us as to what it takes to be a winner."

The next weekend, during a preseason game between Washington and Baltimore, a message recorded earlier by Lombardi was played over the public address system. The words, touching in their directness and simplicity, moved all who heard them.

"I owe most everything to football, and I have never lost my respect and my admiration, nor my love, for what I consider a great game." He added that "to the winner there is one hundred percent elation, one hundred percent laughter, one hundred percent fun. And to the loser— the only thing left for him is a one hundred percent resolution, and a one hundred percent determination" to become a winner.

He ended with words that he used to measure others, and by his own words, Lombardi certainly proved to be a success. "The quality of any man's life has got to be a full measure of that man's personal commitment to excellence and to victory, regardless of what field he may be in."

In commemoration of football's greatest coach, the award for winning the Super Bowl is known as the Vince Lombardi Trophy.

Lombardi continues to influence his former players, even though he passed away many years ago. Jerry Kramer, a successful businessman, found that most people in his field try to make things easier by taking short cuts. Not him.

"I've got an edge, because whenever I'm tempted to screw off, to cut corners, I hear that raspy voice saying, 'This is the right way to do it. Which way are you going to do it, mister?'"

Willie Davis built his own thriving business. He said that, "I jog in the morning, and there are days when I wake up and I don't feel like getting up and crawling into the office. Then I think, 'What would Lombardi do?' I get up and out of bed, and I throw on my sweats and I jog."

Lombardi would have smiled at these words, content that his players had listened.

STATISTICS

Vincent Thomas Lombardi

YEAR	TEAM	WON	LOST	TIED
1942	St. Cecilia	6	1	2
1943	St. Cecilia	11	0	0
1944	St. Cecilia	10	0	1
1945	St. Cecilia	5	3	2
1946	St. Cecilia	7	3	0
TOTALS		39	7	5
1959	Green Bay	7	5	0
1960	Green Bay	8	4	0
1961	Green Bay	11	3	0
1962	Green Bay	13	1	0
1963	Green Bay	11	2	1
1964	Green Bay	8	5	1
1965	Green Bay	10	3	1
1966	Green Bay	12	2	0
1967	Green Bay	9	4	1
TOTALS		89	29	4
1969	Washington	7	5	2

Postseason Games

1960	NFL CHAMPIONSHIP: Lost to Philadelphia, 17-13
1961	NFL CHAMPIONSHIP: Defeated New York Giants, 37-0
1962	NFL CHAMPIONSHIP: Defeated New York Giants, 16-7
1965	WESTERN CONFERENCE PLAYOFF: Defeated Baltimore Colts, 13-10;
	NFL CHAMPIONSHIP: Defeated Cleveland Browns, 23-12
1966	NFL CHAMPIONSHIP: Defeated Dallas Cowboys, 34-27;
	SUPER BOWL I: Defeated Kansas City Chiefs, 35-10
1967	WESTERN CONFERENCE PLAYOFF: Defeated Los Angeles Rams, 28-7;
	NFL CHAMPIONSHIP: Defeated Dallas Cowboys, 21-17;
	SUPER BOWL II: Defeated Oakland Raiders, 33-14

VINCENT LOMBARDI:
A CHRONOLOGY

1913   Vincent Thomas Lombardi born on June 11.

1933–
1937   At Fordham University, becomes one of the "Seven Blocks of Granite."

1942   Becomes head football coach at St. Cecilia; Son, Vincent, Jr. is born.

1947   Named assistant coach at Fordham; daughter, Susan, is born.

1949   Named assistant coach at West Point.

1954   Named assistant coach with the New York Giants.

1956   Helps Giants win the NFL Championship with a 47-7 win over the Chicago Bears.

1958   Giants lose in sudden death to the Baltimore Colts in a classic battle.

1959   Signs a five-year contract with Green Bay.

1960   Packers lose to the Philadelphia Eagles in Lombardi's first championship game.

1961   Packers trounce the New York Giants, 37-0 in NFL championship game.

1962   Packers defeat New York Giants, 16-7, for Lombardi's second straight title.

1965   Packers defeat Cleveland Browns, 23-12, for Lombardi's third NFL title in five years.

1967   Packers beat Kansas City Chiefs, 35-10, in Super Bowl I.

1968   Packers beat Oakland Raiders, 33-14, in Super Bowl II for his third straight title; resigns as Green Bay head coach.

1969   Signs as head coach and general manager of the Washington Redskins.

1970   Dies of cancer in Washington, D. C.

SUGGESTIONS FOR FURTHER READING

Berger, Phil. *More Championship Teams of the NFL.* New York: Random House, 1974.

Clary, Jack. *Pro Football's Great Moments.* New York: Bonanza Books, 1983.

Klein, Dave. *The Vince Lombardi Story.* New York: Lion Books, 1971.

Kramer, Jerry, editor. *Lombardi: Winning is the Only Thing.* New York: Thomas Y. Crowell Company, 1970.

Liss, Howard. *Playoff!: Professional Football's Great Championship Games.* New York: Delacorte Press, 1966.

O'Brien, Michael. *Vince: A Personal Biography of Vince Lombardi.* New York: Quill Books, 1987.

Schoor, Gene. *Football's Greatest Coach: Vince Lombardi.* Garden City, New York: Doubleday & Company, Inc., 1974.

ABOUT THE AUTHOR

John F. Wukovits is a teacher and writer from Trenton, Michigan who specializes in history and sports. His work has appeared in over twenty-five national publications, including *Sports History* and *Hoop.* His books include a biography of the World War II commander, Admiral Clifton Sprague, and he earlier wrote biographies of Barry Sanders, Jesse James, and Wyatt Earp for Chelsea House. A graduate of the University of Notre Dame, Wukovits is the father of three daughters—Amy, Julie, and Karen.

INDEX

```
J            Wukovits, John F.,
B              1944-
Lombardi
W            Vince Lombardi.
```

DATE			